The sport of parenting

The sport of parenting

A lovely little book of reflections and art.

Written and illustrated by Oyuki Aguilar
Designed by Jadyn Aguilar

Balboa Press books may be ordered through booksellers or by contacting:

Balboa Press
A Division of Hay House
1663 Liberty Drive
Bloomington, IN 47403
www.balboapress.com
1 (877) 407-4847

Illustrated by Oyuki Aguilar and Jadyn Aguilar.

ISBN: 978-1-5043-4753-2 (sc)
ISBN: 978-1-5043-4754-9 (e)

Print information available on the last page.

Balboa Press rev. date: 1/14/2016

BALBOA.
PRESS
A DIVISION OF HAY HOUSE

A gift of moments, hopes and dreams
that parents share

especially for you

with love,

Gazpoli Girls

Triumph

A bouquet of praise
  for you
    with joy

on this most grand occasion.

We commemorate today,
the moment you decided to become

a parent.

You are a true athlete in the sport of rearing
and you're reaching the finish line just fine.

The results come in,
  you are in the lead
    with your blissful children
      and the power of self-worth.

We award you

with a blue ribbon for your hardship,
a diploma for your pain and guilt,
a medal for your sacrifice,
and a trophy for your success.

Applause and loud cheers for you on your journey
and all the milestones you go through,

on this marvelous triumphant expedition

of training and producing beautiful
and perfectly imperfect humans beings.

Waiting. . .

My miniature

   let us meet at dusk,

that time of day
when the sun plays artist
and dyes the town of marigold.

Then,
let us delight ourselves with the anticipation
that our eyes and hands will soon fix.

While we wait,
you can play to my heartbeat,
I can look for your knee,
you can wait for my voice,
I can wait for your kick.

When we should tire,

   may the night's somnolent riches take us in
      cradled by Vivaldi's Violins

and grow...

just grow.

Me in love with you
and you...
in my pond full of miracles.

Origin of a star

In the tiny cosmos of my womb,

what a spectacle it must have been,
  that first source of light,
    that nebula,
      that origin of a star.

You must have been so frightened
witnessing all those brilliant clouds and
blurred shapes,
for much fear lies in the great unknown.

And then the cold,
I apologize for the unexpected cold dry air
but it was time to meet you.

This world can be so abrupt,
  so uncertain
    and yet, full of many glorious things.

Very soon you were bundled up
and placed in my embrace.

I spoke to you,
perhaps the only familiar sound in your short little history.

Then, Serenity took you by the hand when you recognized my voice and the
music in my chest.

Welcome to the universe my child,
this vast expanse of space, time and mater;
where my love for you predominates above everything else.

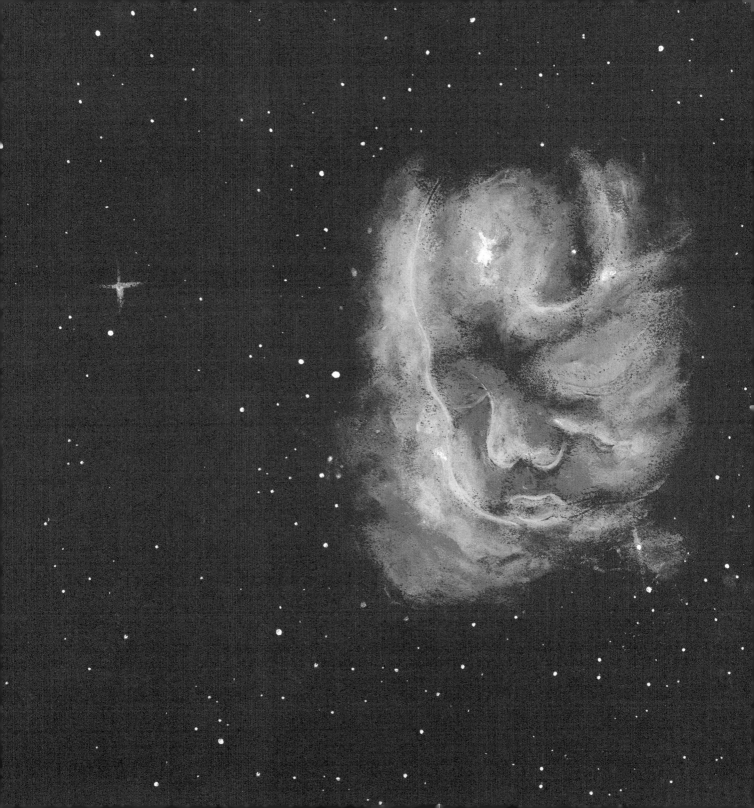

You gave me so much
when you let me hold you.

I am deeply grateful.

I treasure our time together like a valuable artifact,
  like a marble sculpture,
    perfect and eternal.

Your fuzzy head on my chin,
your trusting cheek sleeping on my shoulder
and your light fragrant breath.

I could have held you like this forever.

A minuscule vessel,
  such an immense presence
    that taught me more about concepts like:

      humility,
      intimacy,
      vulnerability.

You,
petite you,
are the patron of my better qualities,
the woodworker of my patience,
the ambassador of my drive for passion
in everything that I do.

Diapers

Today's forecast is
sunny and warm with a chance of perfect
to begin preparations for diaper graduation. Yessss.

Beginning with the proper attire:
one very long t-shirt
and nothing more.

This occasion asks for minimal clothing
to promote self control
and the freeing sensation of ventilation.

You will probably not get it the first time
but...
try and try we will
until you get it right

and your teachers stop dropping hints
   that I'm slacking off
      and that you're really milking the sweet life
        of going whenever
           wherever.

Yes, today is the perfect day to celebrate the toilet jubilee,
   if we do not succeed, then perhaps tomorrow
      or the day after...

It's the perfect time anyways.
   Your life will improve for it,
   that I promise.

Bath time

The loose paint in my bathroom wall
reveals shapes of pirate ships and treasure maps
on the plaster.

For some...
   could be a problem.

For me...
Child's art.

They are decorations made by loving osmosis
provided by my children's tiny bodies.

Just look at them
interrupting that peaceful water.
   They lift it,
      twirl it,
         shake and dance it.

They break all the laws of hydrodynamics
amid their jingle bell laughs.

And like little scientists, they also enjoy to test soap's viscosity:
using their small hopeful breaths
they blow much happiness into those multi colored spheres.

What grandeur is contained in a single bubble.

What magnificence radiates within that miniature wet freedom.

First day of school

I left you that radiant new morning
on the doorstep
where you looked flawlessly angelic.

But soon you became brazen
and entered a state of terror,

they took you.

I turn around
and walk back to my car a sunken wreck,

I can hear you screaming for me.

I left you
and my soul plummeted with hatred.
   Then I cursed as I drove away.
      I cursed at myself and the process of

         the uncivil rapture,
         the maddening tear,
         the unnatural separation
         of a perfectly divine alliance.

Yes,
I left you.
I wish I could tell you
it will not happen again,
   but such is life, my brave little warrior,
      a series of exercises
         of letting go....

Please don't spit out your vegetables

When it's vegetable time,
I imagine we are in a western movie
and you and I are enemies
who are about to engage in a duel.

Each one
is at an opposite end of a dirt road,
some crows are cackling in the far,
one or two tumbleweeds rolling by.

Our stares lock,
and you look at me with skepticism
while in my eye you can see I'm figuring out victory tactics.

Telepathy does not work
nor do explanations about nutrition
so I resort to song and mimics
    but to no avail.

You just hold on to your guns,
    you tighten your lips,
        you spit out what little gets in.

 I sigh...

It seems you win again partner.
    Till we meet again,
        I now go to fix a new batch of your favorite things.

Carpool

I feel some innocent glances
spying on me
through my rear view mirror.

Little gazes starving for novelty
and determined to find answers.

I ask out loud: "what are you thinking?"

they just smile

with those sun kissed smiles
beaming with expectations.

I'm not always allowed into that kingdom.

Such a privilege to be let in.
That land of games and fears,
of trolls and feats,
of happy ever afters and make-believes.

For now,
I just pretend to be a coachmen
instructing it's white horses to hurry
so we can arrive at paint class before 4 p.m.

Or else,
become a tired raggedy mom with a pumpkin on her hand
in the middle of the street.

Accidents

Perhaps the greatest thing
to come out of your fractured clavicle
was your X rays;
a picture that let me take a peek at your inside.

I marveled for hours

at your lovely skeletal system.

From the top of your perfect vertebrae,
down to your spacious rib cage,

that fascinating enclosure
where instead of holding a canary
you hold my whistling heart on a perch.

And there it was,
your snapped little twig and my bent spirit.

You cried tears
while I cried helplessness.
How was I supposed to know kicking a ball
on the grass would lead us here?

But we quickly healed and are ready for our next feat,
a broken heart, a severed dream, a sprained wish.

There are no x rays for these,
but we will overcome them just the same.

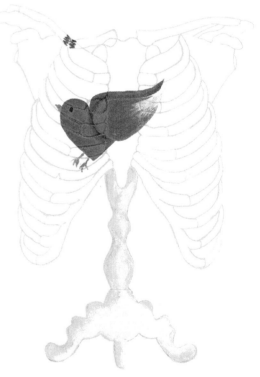

Board games

You and I are on a high speed race.

One where we run fast on a snowy field with candy cane pine trees,
cross a bridge over a colorful gumdrop meadow,
go through a rainbow lollipop forest.

Then you come to a halt.
You are stuck in a sugary swamp
and I pretend not to look
as you manipulate the spinner in order to win.

You lovely little cheat.

I love observing you glitter with triumph.

However,
I enjoy greater pleasure witnessing your loss,
for I know then, you have acquired the prize of tolerance.

Board games in a way, prepare you for everything else.
   Along the way
      we lose many things...
         toys, money, keys, friends, loves, time
            even our minds.

But so many other options we gain:
play a new game, a different game, with different people, with new strategies
and new exciting emotions...

      Who's next?

Loose tooth

Now that your tooth
is about to fall off
I feel my right arm will fall with it.

You are becoming independent so fast
that you need me less and less
just like those baby teeth.

And you are so gleeful about it too.

May you always be this cheerful

when parting with unnecessary things
like:

   Bad habits and bad attitudes,
     negative thoughts,
       judgmental people,
         pier pressure,
           dishonest friends,
             toxic environments.

That way,
your smile will keep its sprightly brilliance
and you will remain genuine and pretty and amazing,
regardless of that bat cave and grand canyon of a gap.

Bedtime stories

I did not know I could speak pirate
but I can.

I can also do witch,
monster,
English rabbit,
and dainty princess.

I specialize now a days in special effects
such as underwater conversations,
explosions,
animal calls,
various train noises and other forms of transportation.

Plenty of dramatization is the key
to make a bedtime story successful.

I take storytelling very seriously.

I enjoy diving in the seas of those beautifully decorated pages
and I become its picturesque characters.

I do it and wear it all;
  the boots and hooks,
      the hats and capes.

While you wear that amazement in your look
and that enormous wonder filled grin on your face.

Philosophy at midnight

No, cake does not have the same amount of vitamins as vegetables.

Yes, I will keep your tooth from being stolen by the tooth fairy so you can take it to school to show your friends.

No, your brother will not develop boobies like daddy if he diets and exercises.

No, tomorrow is not your birthday and yes, you can change your birthday party theme AGAIN.

No, most of us can't control our dreams. Everybody has nightmares once in a while. They are scary but few and harmless, and I am here.

Yes, there are bad people in the world, but they are scarce. There are far more good people. We just have to watch out for those few mean ones, because they can make plenty of harm.

No, I am not getting old just yet; not for a long time.
Yes, I will die one day, but not for a long time (hopefully).

No, you are not getting old just yet, there are many years to come.
Yes, eventually you will die... but not for a very very very long time.

Let us not worry about this tonight, instead let us think about what we can control, like where to go, what to play and sing and figure out how to be more happy.

Try worrying about that other stuff at noon please.

Good night.

Selective hearing impairment

Fine,
maybe you did not hear me the first time I called you
  or the second
but I think you heard me the third
  and fourth;
I'm not sure, you could have been spaced out in your inner world.

You definitely heard me the fifth time because I counted to three
and I raised my voice a little bit.

Now I'm pretty sure I captured your attention because I yelled
and a surprised stillness overtook you.

I detest so much this ignoring game you play,
  I don't understand the rules to it,
    I don't know what the objectives are
      because nobody ever wins.

Well; I guess you win
  when I get irritated,
    then I tag you and I end up annoying you too,
      it all finishes when you sulk and I have a bad mood.

There are important lessons to be rescued here by both players,
like continually exercising self restraint, respect and patience.

Now that I think about it, it's not a complete waste of time
and energy after all.

Sleepless nights

I am fencing with the forces of Morpheus
to stay vigilant of your temperature.

At the same time
you practice karate with your nemesis:

The Evil Viruses.

They are invaders and thugs
that have given us long years in battles
and countless sleepless nights.

Tonight
they interrupt our peace again,
once again they will leave and vanish defeated.

Take this art of combat and defense
and use it well on:
people who want to harm you in any way
and anything or anyone you consider unjust
  or unequal,
    sexist
      or racist;

hold your fort strong like tonight.
Preserve your integrity, your health and your bliss
at all costs.

The beach

Let us take a break
from these clay and macaroni craft filled days
and search for liberty
at the beach;
and we won't come back until we find it.

We will look over powdered seashells and corals,
under naked vibrant skies
next to roaring gushing waters
and beyond the infinite horizon.

I found mine

in a couple of gorgeous dwarf silhouettes
running towards me
with a glitter sprinkled ocean in the background
and totem pole clouds above.

Let's collect conches filled with hermit laughter,
marvel at the joyful tentacles of the anemone,
build tall impressive love castles,
play toss and catch with happiness.

Finally... enjoy the day's closing with an orange lush ceremony.

Pick up all of our equipment, our memories, chairs and leftover treats.

Go home weaving a lifelong picture album in our dream catcher spirits.

Gold rush

Let science fascinate you, child.
The natural world is so enticing.
There are amazing places abundant in valuable information
to enrich your mind with wisdom and your heart with humility.

Begin by enjoying the earth,
the soil,

your origin.

That matter which everyone and everything is made out of;
enjoy your geology.

Go into the museums and mines,
those dark fresh corners
where precious metals are found
along with glaring gems and minerals that can mesmerize anyone,
just like your interior.

But be careful not to confuse riches with costly shiny things
like the greedy ones,
rather learn to find the real treasures
in nature, in books, in music, in the pure souls of beautiful people.

I myself, keep my bounty in a box containing hospital baby bracelets, first
locks of hair, baby teeth and handmade cards with crooked hearts and stick
figures hugging; I also receive little kisses and grins daily.

I live in such opulence, that I wonder how I managed to stay so modest.

Building blocks

Entropy.
Physicists use this unit of measurement to evaluate chaos.
They say order can not be so
without some disarray behind it.

I appreciate this concept best
when my children dump ALL of their building blocks
on my living room floor
and there isn't a safe space to step on.

But as minutes happily frolic by,
all the scattered debris of colorful cubes and prisms
begin to disappear like magic

and shapes begin to appear and grow.

Odd shapes,
cool shapes,
unforgettable shapes

like that submarine train
perfect for an underwater railing system of course
and that cubist teddy bear
or how about that skyscraper hospital with all those beds.
Amazing.

So when I see my house imploding,
it's ok, it's only a little entropy.

Evaluation

I think next week on Thursday
we should have a parent evaluation.

I would very much like to know
how I am performing as your caretaker in various categories.

I would appreciate a filled multiple answer format
where I am being graded on:
    Physical appearance,
    hygiene,
    punctuality,
    nutrition in prepared meals and snacks,
    school activities,
    extra curricular activities,
    homework tutor,
    social ambassador and play date planner,
    problem solving skills,
    anger management,
    disposition and happiness levels.

No matter how I may seem,
I am so fulfilled and happy with you in my life.
Most nights, my last thought before I go to dream of you... Is:

  Am I doing a good job?
    Are you growing happy and healthy and civil?

Because being your mom,
is the most important job of all.

Parent evaluation

Kids, help mommy or daddy find out how they are doing by adding a checkmark.

How are mom or dad doing?	Good	So-so	Bad
Physical appearance			
Hygiene			
Punctuality			
Nutritious meals and snacks			
School activities			
Extra curricular activities			
Homework tutor			
Social ambassador			
Play date planner			
Problem solving skills			
Anger management			
Disposition			
Happiness			

Guinea pig

Last week,
Monday morning
you could not get yourself to dress on your own to go to school
even though you do it merrily for parties and outings.

You could not brush your teeth,
eat your breakfast
or even hold still while I brushed your hair.

And then you broke the news...
You want a Guinea Pig.

Interesting.

You cannot hold yourself to be responsible for simple everyday tasks
and yet somehow you are prepared enough to take care of
a defenseless creature.

I'm sorry,
I'm just not convinced that is a wise petition.
You will have to prove yourself worthy and convince me, please.

Today, with a huge smile
you woke up, ate your breakfast, cleaned your room,
got dressed and held still while I brushed your hair.
It's impressive how a little perspective can get a child a Guinea Pig.

Astronaut

Big box of crayons is out
and you color nothing but rocket ships
and planets.
"It is official" you say,
today, you want to be an astronaut.

And where you see asteroids,
I see an opportunity to expand your mind.
I will take advantage of this newly found interest in space
and use it
to go stargazing at night,
toy with fun facts about our solar system,
even visit a space shuttle at the science center.

You see,
it is at exciting times like these when we reap our knowledge.
Curiosity opens a portal in our intellect and waves of information flow in
like a sweet mist.

We grow, we evolve, we become greater.

Last week I myself wanted to be a tourist in Italy,
so I learned plenty, of its art, its fiords and hot springs.
Beautiful spaces designed by both human beings and nature,
places to visit one day with you.

But today,
I just want to be your mommy,
I just want to learn more about you.

no santa

I know you would like to believe in all of them,

just like your friends and relatives
that hold on to their stories and expect their magical gifts.

But they simply do not exist.

There is no such thing as Santa Claus,
no tooth fairy
or Jack Frost.
There is absolutely no Easter bunny,
no sandman,
cupid or garden gnomes.

However,

there are your grandparents to give you love and chocolates,
aunts and uncles that will buy you toys,
friends to play pretend with
and godparents to shower you with joy.

Then there is your daddy who will work to give you everything he can
and your mommy... to guard you and kiss your cares away.

So if you are going to be grateful with characters
and hand them out your heartfelt thank yous,
then count your true blessings
and may I suggest you acknowledge
the real heroes of your years.

Gloom

You can really contract gloom from a rainy day.

There is something very depressing about all that grey
and those dripping sounds of gutters.
It all echoes loudly inside of me and I feel soaked with guilt.

In my thought puddles,
I painfully keep replaying yesterday morning
when we had our disagreement, our power struggle.

There was no room for negotiation and no resolutions could be found.
You were rejecting all of my offers then began to order me around with your
doll size arrogance.
My patience washed away from me gradually
until anger overtook me.

I roared at you in a way that I could have produce lightning.
I demanded respect, but sadly, it was all said in a disrespectful tone.
Now, I stupidly console myself by thinking I'm preparing you for the harsh
world outside, but I'm wrong to burst out that way.
I'm the grownup, I have wisdom and tools, and I am a disappointment.

I wait for my pardon,
I also wait for a new sunny opportunity where
I can do better.

I wait for your forgiving look
and your rainbow smile.

The invasion of artwork

Our house has turned into a museum of art.

You will find the artistic works
scattered throughout the gallery,
mounted on the refrigerator, the walls, the doors,
over the computer, on the bookshelf, in drawers
and tucked away by bulk in closets.

On this particular morning
I opened my notebook to write to you
and discover no blank page available.

Even more beautiful that my play of words:
  your artwork.

Each page is surprisingly and exquisitely decorated.
There are houses filled with stick figures holding hands and kittens,
smiley flowers and hearts in playgrounds with swings
and in every one of them, a sun that looks more like a sea urchin.

My favorite one is this one;
a depiction of me with your baby brother in my belly and next to me a crib
where you lay, covered with a blanket, drinking a bottle.

Your limitless imagination placed us in the past, an important moment for
you, a happy memory.
  I really hope you are living this happy little life you draw, my love.

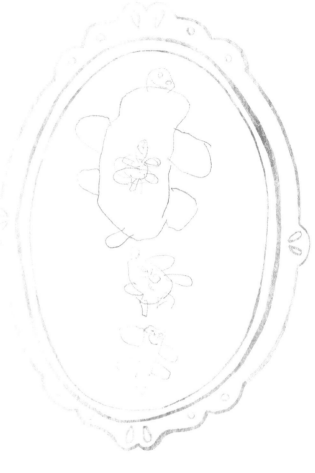

Mommy's resort

Welcome to mommy's resort
a piece of children heaven where all of your needs are met and more.

Here in mommy's resort
we have numerous amenities
such as outdoor playground,
bubble baths,
cable and internet,
five star (made out of construction paper of course) restaurant
and recreation space (my living room.)

Yes, here in mommy's resort
we pamper you and cater to your every need
  any day,
    anytime.

No, we don't need to sleep,
what is that for?

No, no, here you are treated like royalty
because your satisfaction is our priority.

So come and take advantage of our outstanding services
or we will pay for your therapy.

We hope you have a wonderful time here,
at mommy's resort,
because after all, you did not ask to be born.

Date night

I get so tired sometimes
of all the activities,
not you.

I feel the need to return to my grown up roots,
a space to reconcile
with myself and my other passions;
yes, I have other passions besides being a mother.

But just before I walk out the door to do so,
you glance at me with those sad solitaires
and tell me you are going to miss me
while performing an award winning tear jerking role.

I confess, I walk out with a little guilt.
Sometimes a lot, to be sincere.
And I do miss you too,
   very much.

But very importantly, we need not forget who we are
or loose ourselves in one role.

Enjoy being many things...

A son or daughter, a sibling, a friend, a student, an athlete,
activist, employee, tutor or partner.
   And better yet,
      enjoy being you with yourself.

Wishful thinking

In the time it takes me to exhale,
you will have become
a beautiful and glistening adolescent.

And the catalog for this next life's season
will feature
difficult situations and worrisome scenarios
that nurture my insomnia constantly.

You will mostly be looking for your own identity
and will encounter many attractive options of fashion,
thoughts and conduct.

But consider this:

Create your own criteria.

Independent thinkers
are brave pathfinders and free spirits
that constantly question the status quo,
they are not easy followers of fads and popular beliefs.

They soar above all the repetitive craziness that sometimes hurts humanity
more than improve it.

Be your own original design,
and I will love you proudly for it.

Diversity

There is a whole generous world out there,
far outside our community.
Our globe,
it is a great teacher, a warm nurturer, a defenseless giant.

Get to know It and you will find

many ecosystems of
deserts, lakes and meadows,
mountains, beaches and glaciers.

Old cities,
  new cities
    with different people,
      with different customs
        and different foods.

Strange music,
  beautiful music,
    exotic animals,
      breathtaking works of architecture and art.

Explore, learn and appreciate it all.

Be grateful and greedy of this giant's offerings;
for It is old and wise, smart and most beautiful of all.

Inheritance

I do not know if I will have much to leave you
when I have passed on;

any material items or properties anyhow.

What I do know
is that I will have shared with you the best of me.

I leave you so much love,

   the best kind of love,
     the kind only a parent can give.

I leave you my words

   expressed and written.
     I leave you my teachings and opinions of the world.
      My love of nature, art and literature.

and more pleasant memories than unpleasant, I hope.

I believe these things are far more valuable than any amount of money a
bank account can hold.

But above all
I believe in you, you can be happy and wise and loving if you want,
because I did the best that I could
and that is my inheritance.

For my children... Omar and Oyuki.
I love you,
you crazy little things.

Acknowledgements

I am deeply grateful to all of those souls
whose energy help construct my entity.

I thank my children for my inspiration
and my loving husband Omar for his support.

The care of my sister Jadyn
and my amazing parents Hector and Oyuki.

My cheerleaders Ariz, Carolina, Iliana,
Ana, Hugo and Karina.

My contributors Andrés, Gilberto and Luis.

But above all
I humbly honor
the one who created all the beauty in the universe
and designed my heart;
also my guardian angel who moves my pen.

The most important job that I do is being a mom.

Though it is challenging, I find it extremely enlightening and rewarding.
I suppose I enjoy it so much because I have an autoimmune disease:
Multiple Sclerosis, and that helps me put things in perspective.
I constantly picture a future in my children's lives without me and
that drives me to savor each moment I share with them. I always try
to make something special out of the ordinary, so that they will have
a strong love tool to help them cope with life if I'm ever absent.

I live on the west coast, where the weather is always perfect, so my family
and I take advantage of this gift and do plenty of outdoor activities.
Our home is not very big but we do have a very big backyard
and my children spend most of their days playing outside.

I am truly lucky and blessed.

MAMA OKUKÍ PAPKOW

43

CPSIA information can be obtained
at www.ICGtesting.com
Printed in the USA
FSOW03n1449280116
16314FS